Musk-ox, bison, sheep and goat

Illustrations

ISBN-13: 978-1495327957
ISBN-10: 1495327957

Dtp
and
graphic design
Iacob Adrian

MUSK-OX, BISON, SHEEP
AND GOAT

ILLUSTRATIONS

THE BEGINNING OF THE SLAUGHTER . . . . .

IN THE FAR NORTH . . . .

AT BAY . . . .

OUTNUMBERED . . . .

EAST GREENLAND MUSK-OX CALF . . . .

HEAD OF TWO-YEAR-OLD MUSK-OX BULL . . . .

MUSK-OXEN ON CAPE MORRIS JESUP, BROUGHT TO BAY
BY DOGS . . . .

THE AUTHOR'S BARREN GROUND HUNTING KNIFE AND AX

THE BARREN GROUND MUSK-OX — A FULL-GROWN BULL .

FOREFOOT OF BARREN GROUND MUSK-OX . . . .

FULL-GROWN EAST GREENLAND MUSK-OX — ADULT MALE

FOREFOOT OF EAST GREENLAND MUSK-OX . . . .

SKULL OF THE EAST GREENLAND MUSK-OX — FRONT VIEW

SKULL OF THE BARREN GROUND MUSK-OX — FRONT VIEW

SKULL OF THE EAST GREENLAND MUSK-OX — SIDE VIEW .

SKULL OF THE BARREN GROUND MUSK-OX — SIDE VIEW .

MALE YEARLING OF THE EAST GREENLAND MUSK-OX .

ADULT FEMALE OF THE EAST GREENLAND MUSK-OX .

MUSK-OX CALF . . . .

THE LAST OF THE HERD . . . .

Illustrations

PROTECTED . . . .

ROCKY MOUNTAIN SHEEP . . . .

ALERT . . . .

UNDER A HOT SKY . . . .

SURPRISED . . . .

THE SADDLEBACK SHEEP . . . .

ABOVE TIMBER LINE . . . .

THE WHITE GOAT IS AN AGILE CLIMBER . . . .

THE MUSK-OX AND ITS HUNTING

IN THE FAR NORTH

AT BAY

OUTNUMBERED

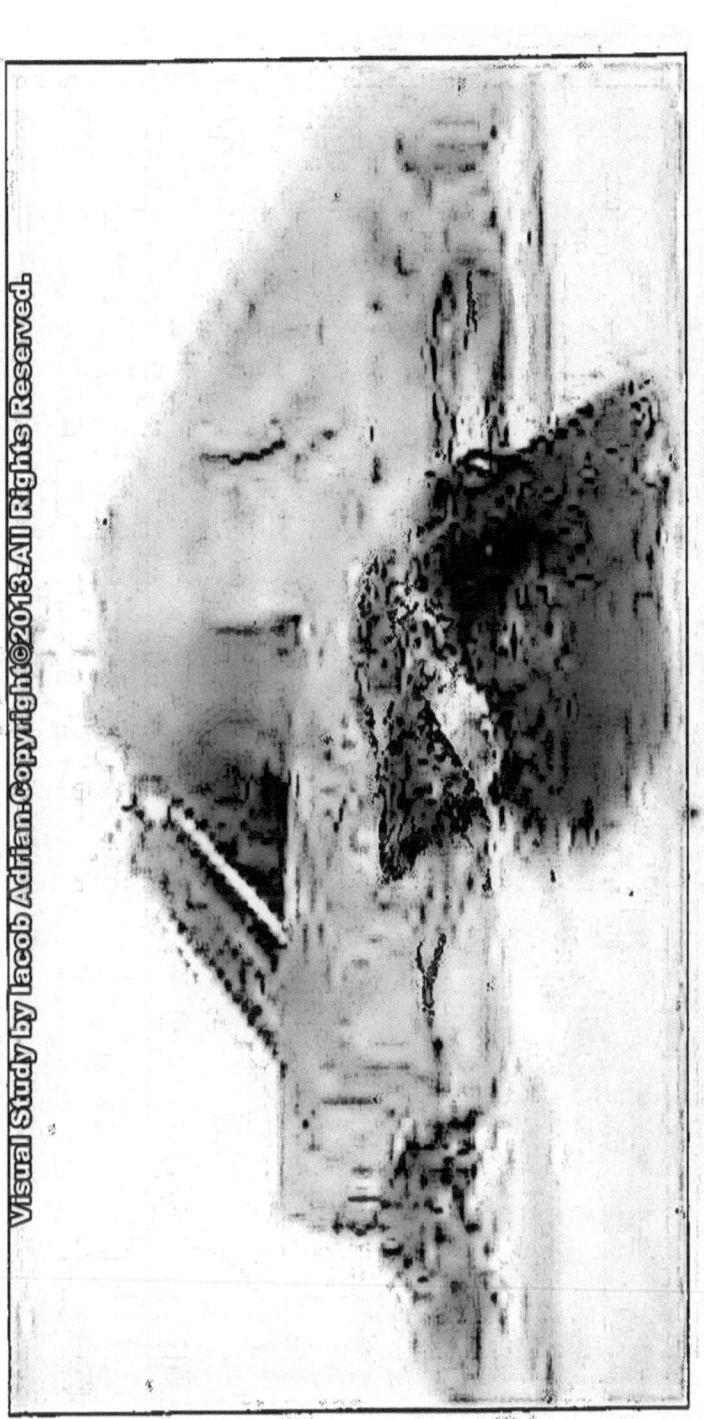

HEAD OF A TWO-YEAR-OLD MUSK-OX BULL.

Killed and photographed in the Barren Grounds by the author. The horns are just beginning to show a downward tendency. Hair over forehead is gray, short, and somewhat curly. The background is the tepee referred to in the text.

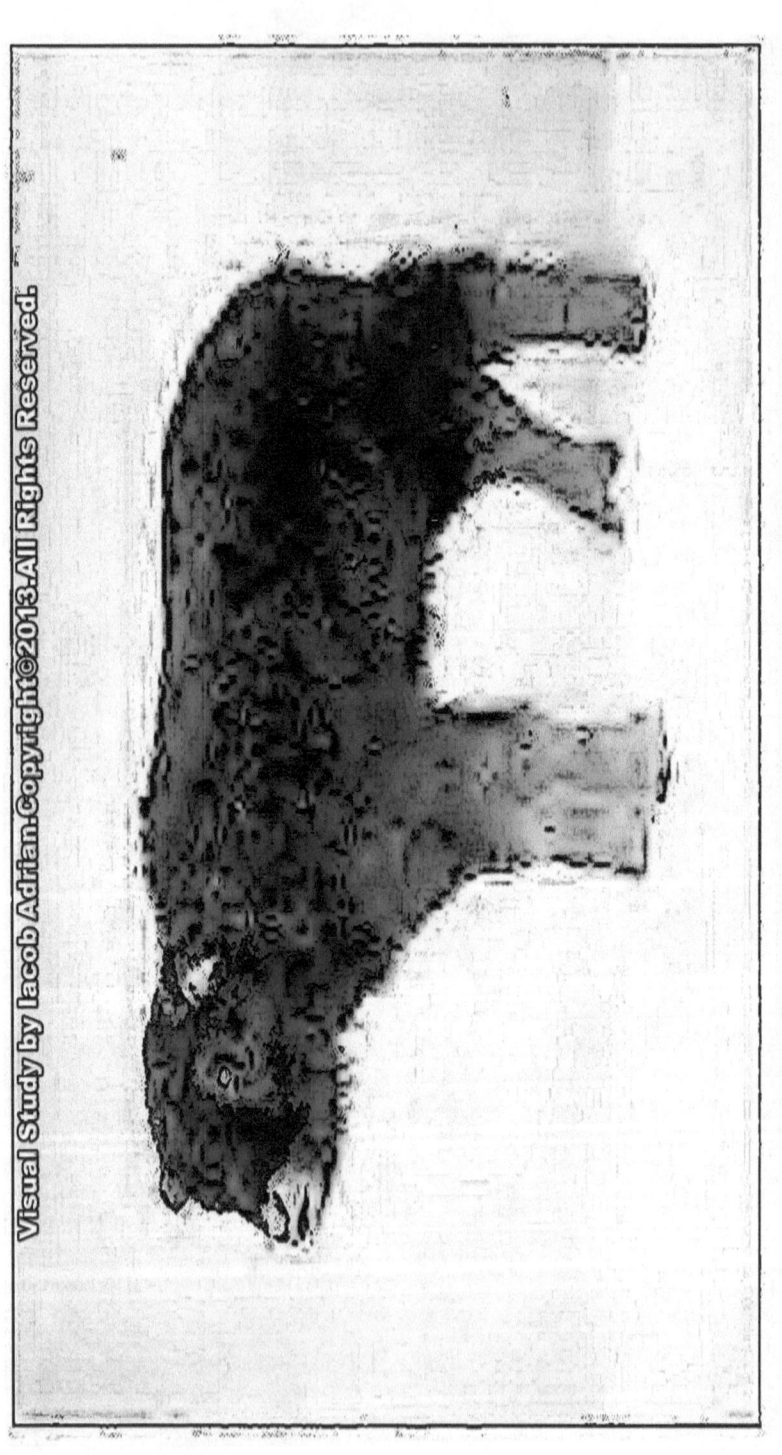

EAST GREENLAND MUSK-OX CALF

Collected at Fort Conger by Commander R. E. Peary. U.S.N. (From a photograph provided by the American Museum of Natural History)

MUSK-OXEN ON CAPE MORRIS JESUP (88° 39' North Lat.). BROUGHT TO BAY BY DOGS
MAY 17TH. 1900

The animals are within a quarter of a mile of the extreme northern limit of the most nor.herly land on the globe. Photograph by courtesy of Robert E. Peary, by whose expedition it was taken.

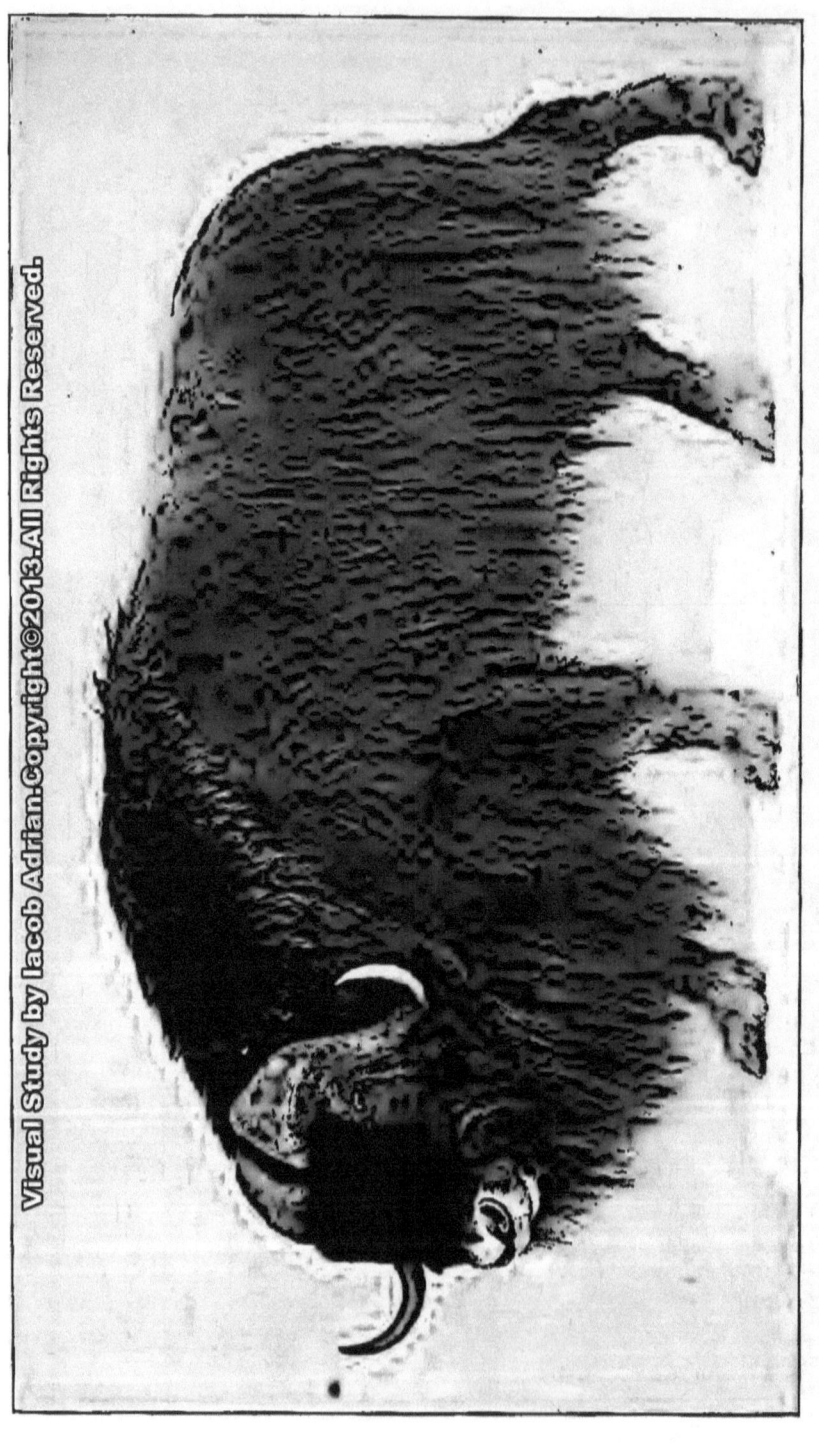

THE BARREN GROUND MUSK-OX — (*Ovibos moschatus*)

A full-grown bull.   (From a photograph provided by the American Museum of Natural History)

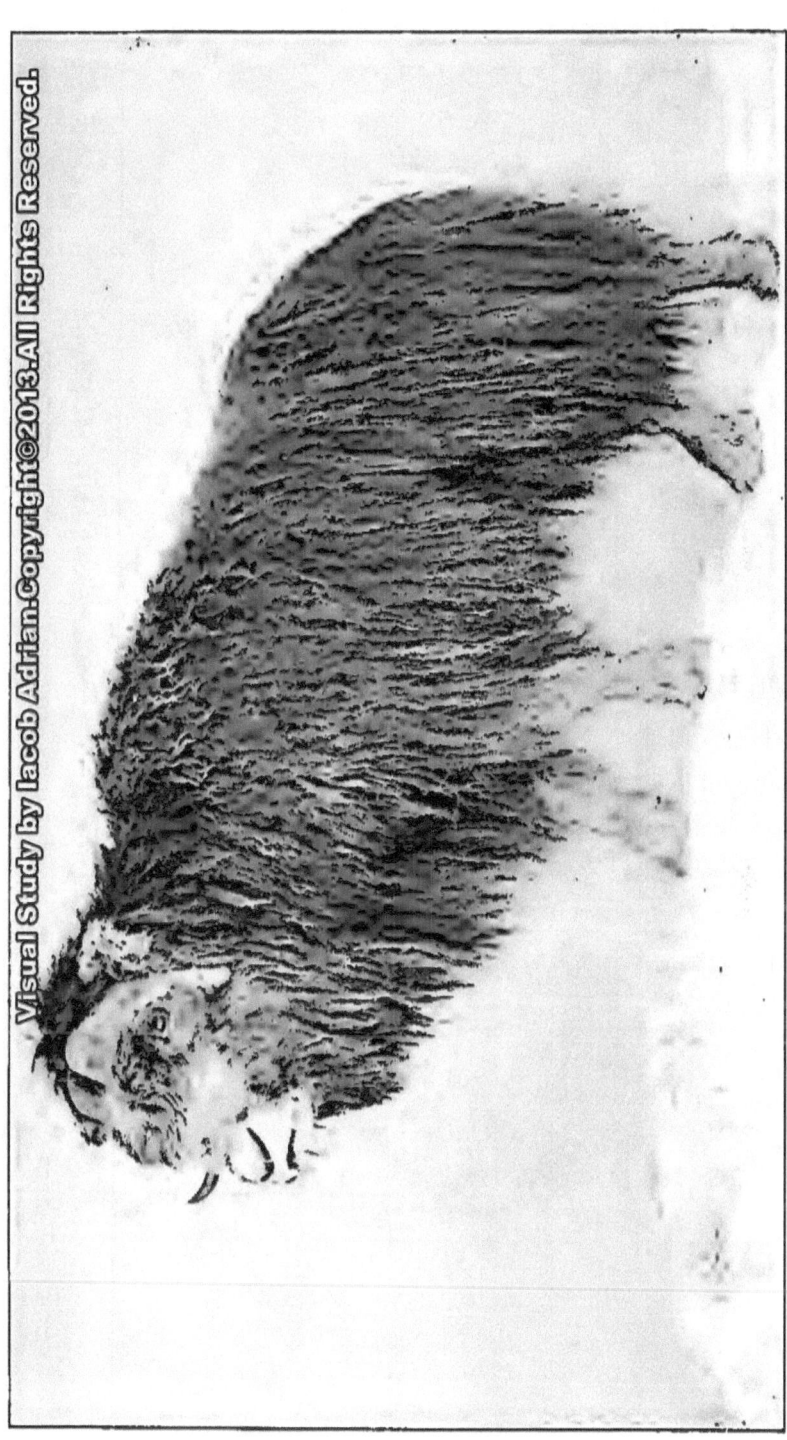

FULL–GROWN EAST GREENLAND MUSK–OX — (*Ovibos Wardi*)

Adult male. (From a photograph provided by the American Museum of Natural History)

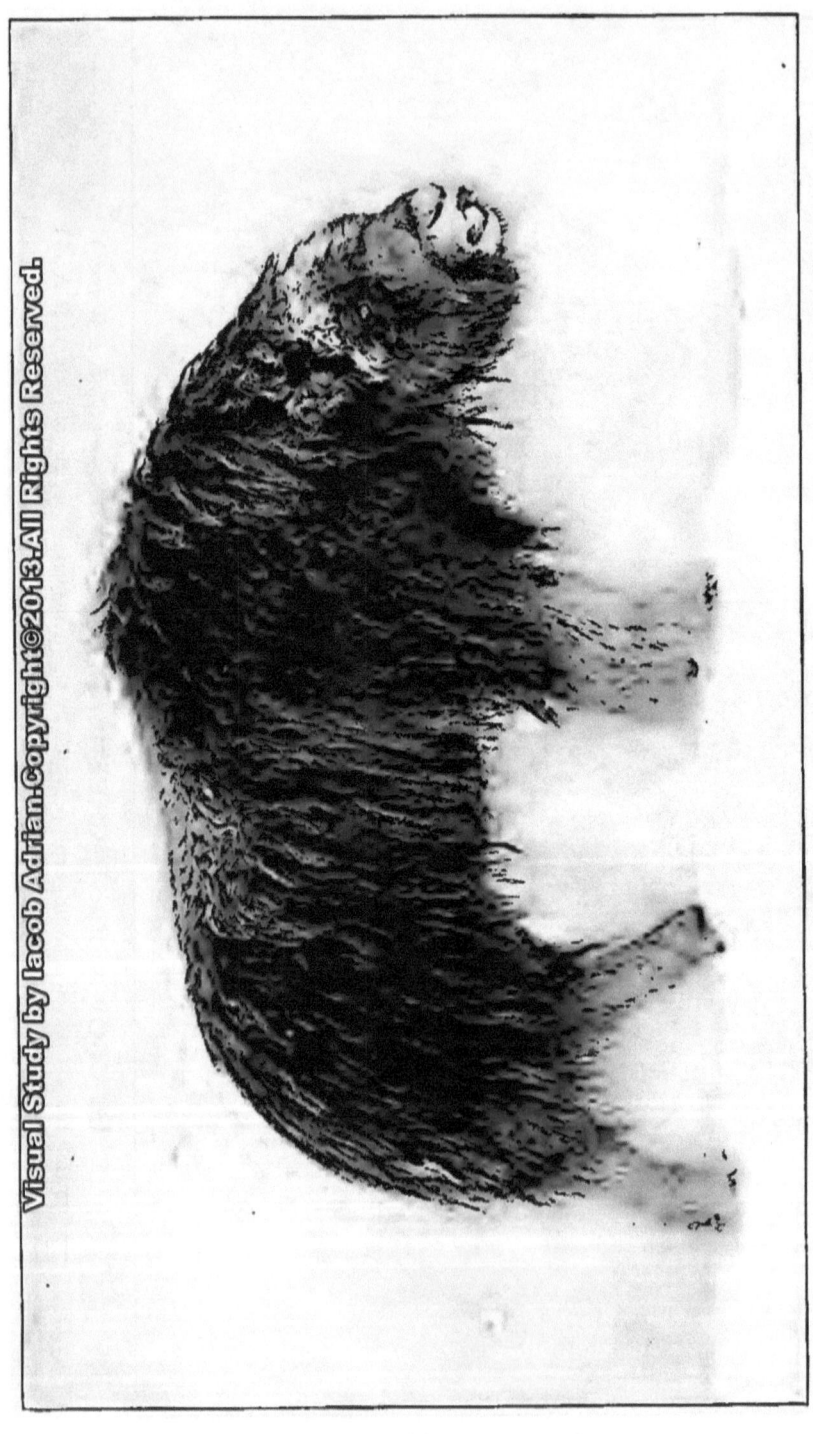

MALE YEARLING OF THE EAST GREENLAND MUSK-OX

(From a photograph provided by the American Museum of Natural History)

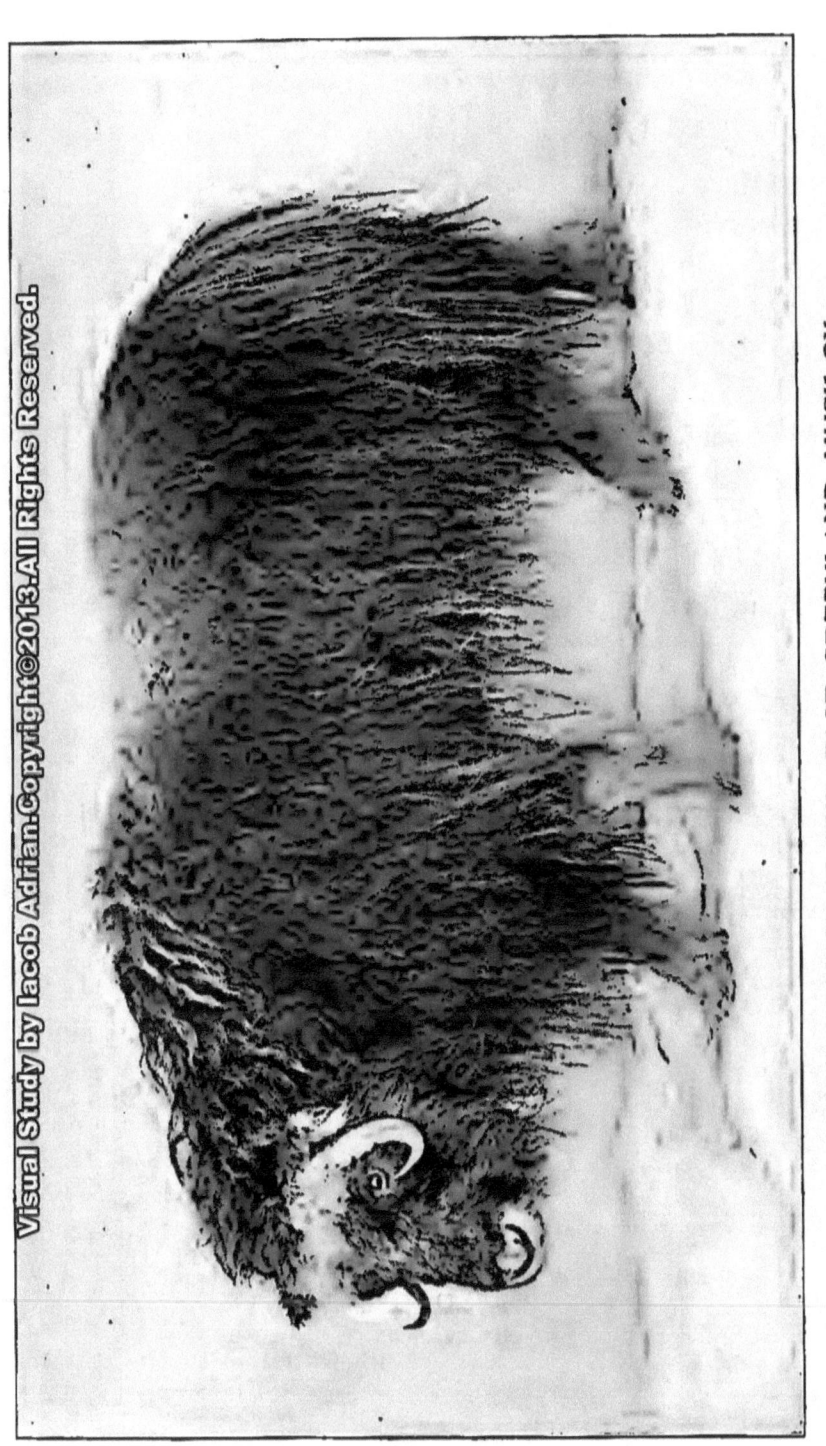

ADULT FEMALE OF THE EAST GREENLAND MUSK-OX

(From a photograph provided by the American Museum of Natural History)

MUSK-OX CALF

This specimen was captured March. 1901. east of Lady Franklin Bay, about 30 miles inland, by Indians sent out by Captain H. H. Bodfish of the whaler *Beluga*. After being exhibited in San Francisco. Chicago. and New York, it was bought by Hon. William C. Whitney, who presented it forthwith to the New York Zoological Society. It died within a few months after. It was the first live member of the musk-ox family ever brought to the United States. (Photograph used by permission of the New York Zoological Society.)

THE BISON

THE LAST OF THE HERD

PROTECTED

THE MOUNTAIN SHEEP: HIS WAYS

ROCKY MOUNTAIN SHEEP

ALERT— (*Ovis stonei*)

UNDER A HOT SKY — (*Ovis nelsoni*)

SURPRISED (White Sheep — *Ovis dalli*)

THE SADDLEBACK SHEEP—(*Ovis fannini*)

THE WHITE GOAT AND HIS WAYS

ABOVE TIMBER LINE

THE WHITE GOAT IS AN AGILE CLIMBER

Bibliographic sources :

Musk-ox, bison, sheep, and goat (1904)

Author:
Whitney, Caspar, 1862-1929;
Grinnell, George Bird, 1849-1938;
Wister, Owen, 1860-1938

Publisher: New York, London, Macmillan